Litur [and Ethics]

by

Oliver O'Donovan

Professor of Moral Theology, University of Oxford
Canon of Christ Church, Oxford

with a Response

by

Michael Vasey

Lecturer in Christian Worship, St. John's College, Durham
Member of the Church of England Liturgical Commission

gb GROVE BOOKS LIMITED
Bramcote   Nottingham   NG9 3DS

CONTENTS

PREFACE

I have in my time written five and a half Grove Booklets, and of those I intended to write five. The story of the half is this:

One day a friend rang and said, 'I've got Ron Sider coming over and I must have someone to debate with him. I've tried the bishop and I've tried everyone else and they're none of them free. Please come and do it; you don't have to prepare. Just sit and listen, and then react for two minutes'. So I went, I sat, I listened, and I reacted. The next thing I knew was that the proofs arrived on my desk.

Perhaps this paper comes into the same category. Colin Buchanan asked me to speak at the twentieth anniversary 'party' for Grove Books in January 1992, which I agreed to do with joy, but without a heavy sense of scholarly responsibility. No sooner had I finished and everyone adjourned to tea than I was asked for my script. Since I had no full script, what follows is the transcribed and edited tape of what I said.

O. M. T. O'Donovan
March, 1993

THE COVER PICTURE
is by Judith Sugden

First Impression April 1993

ISSN 0951-2667

ISBN 1 85174 235 2

FOREWORD

Grove Books began in late 1971, when Julian Charley's commentary on the Anglican/Roman Catholic Agreement on the Eucharist was published by a colleague of his, a fellow member of staff at St.John's College, Nottingham, Colin Buchanan. That private venture was followed by other booklets on Ministry and Worship which appeared monthly during 1972, produced for the most part by a group of enthusiasts who sought to reassert evangelical Anglican interest in those two areas of church life.

Though that group has changed its name, and in part its membership, down the years it is still functioning, though the punishing monthly schedule has been relaxed somewhat. It passed (with wry smiles) the milestone of Tract 90 (a resumé by Colin Buchanan of evangelical Anglican interest in liturgy) and is now well into the hundreds, having spawned along the way a more weighty series of Liturgical Studies, and more specialist series on Pastoral concerns, Spirituality and Evangelism, while the project as a whole weathered commercial problems of its own. Some of the booklets have engaged in controversy, or trodden ground where evangelicals (though perhaps not angels) had hitherto feared to tread, while many have simply offered sound pastoral advice and support.

The first of the daughter series was in fact Ethics, born in 1973 in response to an awareness, expressed (I seem to recall) by Alec Motyer, that evangelicals also needed to reassert their interest in the field of Ethics. The first of that series was a discussion of the then very topical issue of abortion, written by a young tutor at Wycliffe Hall, Oliver O'Donovan, a booklet which is still relevant (as we note in this paper) and which has run into a number of new editions and reprints and is still in print to-day. Oliver is one of a number of authors who cut their teeth, as it were, on a Grove Booklet, but have now graduated to more weighty writing with wider recognition. That was indeed one of the secondary aims of the project: namely, to enable writers for a wider ministry.

It was therefore appropriate that he, now Professor of Moral Philosophy and Canon of Christ Church, Oxford, should be the keynote speaker at the twentieth anniversary gathering of those involved in Grove Books since its inception at St. John's College, Nottingham on 18 January 1992. What follows is an edited version of his lecture and the brief discussion after it. Since he was, as a moralist, challenging liturgists to frame their efforts in particular ways, a response has been included by another Grove author, Michael Vasey, who serves on the Church of England's Liturgical Commission.

G. S. Forster
Convenor, Grove Ethics Group.

1. INTRODUCTION

'Liturgy and Ethics' is a suitable topic, I hope, for this meeting. I speak as a moralist, not as a liturgist, thinking about how the work of moralists and liturgists may converge and how they may, perhaps, work together. I am inspired to think about this by an article published by my old teacher, the late Paul Ramsey, in 1979, also under the title 'Liturgy and Ethics.'[1] If I may, I will begin with a reference to that article. He took his departure from Arthur Cochrane's book *The Church's Confession under Hitler*, and claimed that in three actions of the church, confessing faith, generating new liturgical forms, and embarking on some new witness to Christian welldoing, the crucial question is whether they 'had their inception in the consuming fire of a struggle of the church against itself for itself' i.e. in the *status confessionis*. Without this struggle, Ramsey asserted (slightly polemically), 'those who elect to draw up modern creeds, devise new liturgies and experiments for Christian living . . . turn out to be at best plunderers and looters, or at worst petty pilferers of the Christian tradition.'

I don't know whether the concept of a particular moment of *status confessionis* is a useful one; but I do share the view that ethics, liturgy and doctrine all become impossibly flaccid when the church does not grasp hold of them in the context of its own struggle for gospel integrity, the heavenly warfare in which it is engaged. Liturgy and ethics need each other partly because each of them, left to itself, can lose its sense of the lines of battle. Liturgists can overlook the enormous challenges which confront the witness of the people of God; moralists can cease to measure those challenges against the church's inner life of worship, prayer and bible reading, and so fail to interpret them aright.

A Formed Response to God

The link that Paul Ramsey made between liturgy and ethics was based on a phrase that he found in Karl Barth. Barth spoke about the human response to the divine event as, 'not monotonous, colourless and form-less,' but 'articulated, colourful and contoured.' Not a 'mere point' but a 'formed reference.'[2] A good description, Ramsey thought, of liturgy. But in fact it was offered by Barth as a description of the Christian moral life. Ramsey was not aware that Barth had himself made precisely the same connection in the fragment of IV/4 which was published in English in 1981, two years after Ramsey's essay, under the title *The Christian Life.* There Barth proposed that ethics should be understood as the 'invocation of God,' and he intended to expound the Christian moral life through a clause-by-clause analysis of the Lord's Prayer. The life of the people of God is an active expression of the prayer they are taught to pray.

Something more is at work here than that always possibly reductionist claim, *laborare est orare,* a phrase of which we should, I think, be suspicious. What is added is the statement that the Christian life must be a *reference to the work of God,* a reference that is formed by the work of God to correspond to itself. Our living becomes a mirror of God's action.

[1] *Journal of Religious Ethics* (7/2) 1979 pp.139-171.
[2] Karl Barth, *Church Dogmatics* III/4 pp.17, 18.
[3] Discussed further in Question 1, p.18 below.

Cash it out like this: if you think that morality is what all people of goodwill and commonsense agree on, or if you think that morality is derived from the natural conditions of human life, then you will not link ethics and liturgy, because you will not ask how your active life can express what God has done in Jesus Christ, you will not ask how your prayer can make that same reference as your action has to make, though formed in its own way and in its own terms, and so your prayer will not reflect the same struggle for a true reference on which you have embarked in your life. Your prayer will lack the urgency and immediacy of active discipleship, your discipleship will lack the transcendent reference that ought to be given it by prayer.

Putting Action into Words

Now both liturgy and ethics are concerned with the speech that shapes an action. In a liturgical act speech defines and structures what is being enacted: 'We make this memorial', we say, thereby giving the consuming of bread and wine its intention, its meaning, and its structure, so that it becomes *this act*, a truly liturgical act, and not some other act of eating and drinking. Ethical speech, similarly, is the way in which we structure the moral act. Without speech, without conceptualization, we cannot act, but can only 'behave.' Animals behave, even jellyfish behave. You can write a book on the behaviour of jellyfish, but you cannot write a book on the *activity* of jellyfish, because they do not ask themselves what they are doing. They do not say, 'We make this memorial' or indeed 'We do . . .' anything else. The speech of ethical discourse shapes and gives structure to the action; only because it is formed by speech can our action 'refer', speak back to God's act. Only so can it be an articulate action that offers praise and thanks to God who has acted for us.[1]

Levels of Ethical Discourse

The speech of ethical discourse functions in three ways that I want to distinguish:

First by articulating *basic moral categories*, which relate immediately to the kerygma of the gospel; love, obedience, grace, forgiveness, etc. Those fundamental categories form the patterns in which we think about what we do.

Secondly, by integrating those various categories into a *whole moral vision* in which each is intelligibly related to the others. This vision is shaped by salvation-history, the story of the people of God and of God's acts.

Thirdly, by *interpreting the world* into which we must act in the light of that moral vision. Moral speech 'applies'—not a wholly satisfactory word but it will do—our moral vision to the deliberative questions of action, whether they are about nuclear war or embryo transplants, or whatever it is that the believer is forced to deliberate on in the late twentieth century.

[1] Discussed further in Question 1, p.18 below.

5

To understand what ethics is about, it is important to understand that it functions in these three ways, and cannot function only in one of them, though in any given discussion one may be paramount. Liturgy, I suggest, must follow this sequence of moral speech, from the articulation of basic categories to their integration into a moral vision, and then turning that vision in a kind of searchlight on the world, enabling us to discern where we may put our feet and where we are going.

2. LITURGICAL PREACHING AND ETHICS

Let me try to illustrate this first from the commonest of liturgical acts, which even a moralist may perform, that is preaching. I don't know whether I am on safe ground in declaring that preaching is a liturgical act. In the departments of American seminaries, of course, liturgics and homiletics have to be kept quite separate, so that they can get two appointments and not just one; but for our purposes let us think of preaching as one of the fundamental liturgical acts. Although the speech of preaching is freer and more discursive than other kinds of liturgical speech, I certainly experience it, when I preach, as imposing certain characteristic liturgical restraints. I cannot speak in the pulpit as I speak to a class. The language that I use must in some way be fit for liturgy. I cannot chatter away, as I might in chattering to a friend. The language, the place, the subject: all must give expression to the fact that here the church of Jesus Christ articulates its understanding of the faith and life that has been given to it. Preaching has the task of structuring the way in which the people of God think about their active lives, making those lives a formed reference to God's activity.

A Train of Christian Thought

Taking up the phrase that Barth so happily coined and that Ramsey echoed, I would say that preaching, when it touches on moral or social issues, must not be a 'mere point,' but must be 'articulated, coloured and contoured.' It has to trace a train of Christian thought from the gospel itself to the moral categories it implies; and from the way in which those categories cohere in the scriptural vision to the intelligibility they give the world we have to act into.

Working out how one preaches on social, and particularly on political, issues has been a task I have come to late in life. Before I came back to Oxford as a Canon Professor of Moral Theology I had been a moralist, and in a small way a preacher, but I had never made these two enterprises come together. I had burning in my memory the experience of being a graduate student in Princeton University Chapel, and there listening to a pastor who used the pulpit week after week for furious and immoderate attacks on the then President Richard Nixon. So appalled was I by the abuse of the pulpit, (and indeed the unintelligence of the procedure, which rallied support to Nixon's aid from every corner, which in hindsight he did not deserve) that I found myself reluctant to embark on a course of action which might lead me in that direction. Yet I began to find it no longer possible to keep my theological life in two compartments.

These days I end up with some social or moral component in the sermon almost every time. It's not intentional, and occasionally it doesn't happen; but it just turns out this way as I wrestle with the text. I stick closely to the lectionary (more about that in a moment), so that I am less likely to become guilty of riding hobby horses; and I discipline myself to proper exegesis. Then I regard my task as to trace the chain of thought which leads from the lectionary to the world. This is no more than the Puritans did in their highly structured forms of sermon, but with only twenty-five minutes in a Cathedral Mattins you have to be more condensed than the Puritans were!

That way I rarely say more than a fraction of what might be said on any moral or social topic. Usually I get there in the last five minutes, and have spent a long time getting there. And that is what is important, because it is the train of thought into which I want to induct the congregation; so that in the end they will not simply take a position for or against me, but will trace and retrace the train of thought, asking 'How could it be done better, starting from the same point of scripture? What other lines might he have followed? Where might he have gone a different way?' Unless they have it in their power to do this they cannot engage equally as partners with me in the church's task of thinking through the implications of the faith.

On one memorable occasion two ladies from Ulster accosted me angrily after I expressed my doubts about the government's policy of putting a communications ban on *Sinn Fein*. They told me I had stopped them meeting God—a serious charge. All I could claim in my defence was that I showed them *an* authentic Christian train of thought, which still appears to me compelling, which led from the lessons (on the ordination of the deacons and the seventy elders in the wilderness) to the polemical issue that had dominated the news that week. I am confident that the train of thought was exegetically and expositionally sound. The conclusion, of course, was not unarguable—political conclusions rarely are. But the point is not to be politically dogmatic; it is to be theologically honest and open.

As it is with politics, so it is more widely with moral questions. Those of us who care about our responsibilities as moral teachers should, perhaps, ask ourselves the homiletic question: how do I *reach* this topic from the exposition of scripture? Two sentences addressed to some matter of controversy, well prepared for and springing actually from the logic of the homiletic task, can carry as much punch as a half-hour tirade.

Someone recently decided to produce a book of sermons on bioethical topics, and commissioned contributions which, it was insisted, had to be *real* sermons, not didactic lectures or articles. It was an interesting conception, and I would like to see it extended to other moral questions. It is perhaps the supreme test of any Christian moral teaching, whether it could be used as the basis for preaching, without noticeably misappropriating the pulpit to some other kind of enterprise. Only if it could has it achieved its goal, articulating a 'formed reference' which the church must make to God's work in Christ.

3. PRAYING ETHICS

But let us go on to what is more traditionally conceived of as liturgy, and follow the three steps. First of all there is the task of communicating the *basic moral categories* in which the faithful learn to articulate their moral convictions. The faithful will, after all, learn some basic moral categories from somewhere: if they don't learn them from their liturgy, we must ask where will they learn them from. Well, you can guess where from. You only have to listen to Christians talk to come to the opinion that the problem about ethics is not a lack of earnestness or commitment about the moral or the social tasks, but that the moral categories with which their minds are furnished resemble a rubbish dump of contemporary cliché. Tired journalistic turns of phrase come naturally to their lips and they have nothing better to call upon. Small wonder that the more discerning sometimes give up in disgust, deciding that moral questions offer no real scope for a distinctly Christian imagination.

The Place of Ethics

Who can teach them authentic Christian moral categories, if not the liturgists? I share a sadness that I heard expressed among us this morning about the tendency of liturgical reform to weaken the role of liturgy in this regard rather than to strengthen it. The Ten Commandments, for example, have become an archaeological feature in contemporary liturgy. But, of course, it is not just a question of repeating the Ten Commandments. There are many other sources of basic ethical categories which one would like to see exploited in the prayers of the people of God. Why not some of those wonderful lists of virtues from the Epistles, or, of course, the lists of vices, which are sometimes equally striking and memorable?

I am not persuaded that we need to 'revive' the traditionally dedicated tracts of morality in liturgy. Traditionally, ethical teaching has been a preface to confessing sin. It has played the part of Law to Gospel pronounced in the absolution. But think about what might be done, for example, in the post-communion to spread before us the glory of a fully human life into which we are now free to enter. I find the post-communion prayers very flat, a kind of opportunity missed. There is no vision of the life that we are going out to live, rich in possibilities of every kind of action and relationship.

Example 1; Baptism

Let me take a positive example of a case where I think the liturgists have understood what is demanded of them, and that is the baptism service of the Episcopal Church of the United States of America.

First, they have allowed themselves a very full version of the basic baptismal promises, starkly contrasting with the machinegun fire which the ASB offers at that point, and this in order to provide the baptismal candidate and sponsors with a sense of the categorical richness that is at their disposal for thinking about the Christian life.

9

Do you renounce Satan and all the spiritual forces of wickedness that rebel against God?

Do you renounce the evil powers of the world which corrupt and destroy the creatures of God?

Do you renounce all sinful desires that draw you from the love of God?

Do you turn to Jesus Christ and accept him as your Saviour?

Do you put your whole trust in his grace and love?

Do you promise to follow and obey him as your Lord?

Every word there is important. Do people have a concept of *promising*? Do they have a concept of what a *desire* is, and what a *sinful* desire might be? Do they have a sense that there are powers that corrupt, destroy and erode the integrity of fellowship? They are forced to think about all that at baptism.

Not content with that, the Americans have added a further section, which they have called the Baptismal Covenant, in which they have tried to sketch features of the active Christian life to which the new Christian is invited to commit himself or herself.

Will you continue in the apostles teaching and fellowship. and the break-ing of bread and in prayers?

Will you persevere in resisting evil, and whenever you fall into sin, repent and return to the Lord?

Will you proclaim by word and example the good news of God in Christ?

Will you seek and serve Christ in all persons, loving your neighbour as yourself?

Will you strive for justice and peace among all people, and respect the dignity of every human being?

There are problems of detail, I think, and particularly with that last ques-tion; but I cannot help simply admiring the undertaking. Here are liturgists who are more than petty pilferers of the tradition. They are attempting to make something of the occasion, to enrich the Christian's thought about ethics and social commitment right at the heart of the liturgical act, where it counts.

Example 2; Marriage
Take another case, where our own Prayer Book has risen to the challenge, the case of marriage. The preface to the marriage service repeats and

develops a traditional teaching of the church that goes back a millennium and a half about the threefold purposes of marriage: that marriage is for procreation, for remedy against sin, and for the mutual comfort that the one ought to have for the other. In the contemporary marriage liturgy one sees a serious attempt to appropriate this as a memorable piece of marriage catechetics, and to revise it and put it to good service in the modern world.

Yet it is a reflection of the failure of the moralists' teaching of the church that when the liturgists set about this worthy task they showed that they did not understand what the original piece of teaching was about. There are simple mistakes of interpretation in the ASB text, and an obvious omission of one item which had occured in the traditional three and is surely of importance in the modern world too: the power of marriage to provide a sanctifying and disciplining structure for individual holiness.

4. ETHICAL LECTIONS?

We have looked, then, at the communication of basic moral categories. But secondly there is the task of *integrating them into a coherent vision*. If the categories are the furniture of the mind, what we are talking about here is arranging the furniture to make a room. You can put good pieces of furniture together in a way that makes a furniture depository! To make the room, each piece of furniture needs to be in the right relation to the others, it has to be deployed, and so it is with our moral categories. To have a moral vision which will enable us to think out into unfamiliar and strange tasks, we need more than a collection of ideas. They have to interact to make a structured whole.

It is through the reading of scripture that this comes about. Scripture contextualizes these categories into their history, which is the history of God's saving act, and therefore enables our activity to to be a formed reference to that act of God. The moralist, then, has a great stake in the way lectionaries are made. I have great sympathy with the preface Cranmer wrote in the 1549 Prayer Book, from which you might almost conclude that the sole reason for the Reformation was to reform the lectionary. He complained, you recall, of fragmentary and unsystematic reading, so 'that commonly when any boke of the Bible was begon: before three or foure Chapters were read out, all the rest were unread.'

Challenge in the Lectionary

A lectionary that sets out to be protective is a deep disservice to the life of the people of God. Lectionaries become protective when they show anxiety that what we read in Scripture may put a strain on our moral imaginations which may be too much for us. What I want to say is: it is precisely putting our moral imagination under strain, forcing us to come to terms with a vision that is not naturally our own, that teaches us to grow morally.

I happened to be 'in residence' for Advent this year [i.e. December 1991], and so following closely the daily lectionary for Morning and Evening Prayer, and I found in two weeks three occasions on which single verses were deliberately excised, and two on which groups of three or four verses were excised. It may interest you to know what it was that was left out.

Isaiah 45.14. *Thus says the Lord, The wealth of Egypt and the merchandise of Ethiopia, and the Sabaeans, men of stature, shall come over to you and be yours; they shall follow you; they shall come over in chains and bow down to you. They will make supplication to you saying, 'God is with you only, and there is no other, no god beside him.'*

Isaiah 50.11. *Behold all who kindle a fire, who set brands alight! Walk by the light of your fire, and by the brands which you have kindled! This shall you have from my hand: you shall lie down in torment.*

Isaiah 3.16-4.1. *The Lord said: Because the daughters of Zion are haughty ... the Lord will smite with a scab the daughters of Zion. ... In that day the Lord will take away the finery of the anklets ... Instead of perfume there will be rottenness ... Your men shall fall by the sword. ... Seven women will take hold of one man in that day, saying '... take away our reproach.'*

Isaiah 25.10-12. *The hand of the Lord will rest upon this mountain, and Moab shall be trodden down in his place as straw is trodden down in a dungpit.*

I Kings 18.40. *And Elijah said to them, 'Seize the prophets of Baàl; let not one of them escape.' And they seized them and Elijah brought them down to the brook Kishon and killed them there.*

We can only speculate on the different reasons which led the makers of our lectionary to judge that each of these texts put a strain on the imagination of Christ's flock from which they ought to be protected. I find that each of them puts a strain on my imagination, but I do not think that I ought to be protected from it. We must, of course, select. There are ways of selecting that admit us to share the moral vision of the ancient people of God, and there are ways which exclude us from it by falsifying it, and lock us into our cultural prejudices. That is what a bad lectionary can do instead of freeing us. To encounter the disturbing in sacred history is implied in growth in faith. If the charge of plundering or petty pilfering has any force against liturgists or moralists it must surely apply when we take the words with which ancient Israel expressed its moral vision and cut them about with penknives to make them look more like a Victorian religious artefact.[1]

I have in mind especially the literary violence which is done to Psalm 137 when we read it with only one of its two stanzas. It is perfectly obvious that the author intended the two stanzas to stand in sharp contrast to one another, and the first to be experienced in the light of the second. Such a reading lacks integrity simply as a literary exercise; and as a liturgical exercise it should be theologically repudiated.[2]

[1] Discussed further in Question 3, p.18.
[2] Discussed further in Question 5, p.19.

5. THE LITANY OF THE WORLD AS IT IS

The third stage is to engage in an *exploratory encounter with the world.* The Christian moral vision is a searchlight that we have to turn upon the world to interpret it, clarifying the nature and terms of our moral decisions. It might seem that here liturgy can be of little help. But I draw attention to the way in which our prayers and intercessions for the world are structured. To read Cranmer's litany is to get a magnificent portrait of the structure of Tudor society as Cranmer's generation conceived it: the relationships of every class to every other class, the hierarchy, the way in which decisions are taken. You will not get such a picture of our society from the prayers that we have written, because we have thought less about it. We have been less concerned than he was to turn the light of the gospel on our society and ask what we need to pray for.

Paul Ramsey's article focussed with great enthusiasm on an attempt that had been made in the mid-seventies by John Taylor of Winchester to persuade the General Synod to accept for the Alternative Service Book a prayer to be used after an abortion. Ramsey, a passionate and lifelong opponent of abortion, thought that this was an extremely constructive thing to do. The prayer went like this;

> *Heavenly Father, you are the giver of life,*
> *and you share with us the care of the life that is given;*
> *into your hands we commit in trust the developing life*
> *that we have cut short.*
> *Look in kindly judgement on the decision we have made,*
> *and assure us in all our uncertainty*
> *that your love for us can never change.*[1]

If the church marked those abortions it judged defensible with the use of such a prayer, it would teach itself, Ramsey argued, to understand what was at stake in the act of abortion. Simply maintaining a liturgical silence could never teach the church anything.

Occasional Litanies?
One day liturgists may begin to publish 'occasional litanies', rather as they produce 'occasional papers'. While some matter was being publicly debated, these litanies would take the responsibility of exploring the issue in prayer, praying for the good of each concerned party as well as they could discern it. Committing ourselves to pray for things is surely at the heart of committing ourselves to act.

But it would be necessary to pray *for something.* Imagine that a litany had been published by the Church of England on the Gulf War: every actor, every type of situation, every concern, all brought before God. Without jumping to quick judgments and trying to settle the moral issue straight out, we would have made sure that we put ourselves under the discipline of prayer not to omit anything. (There was a letter in the press just before

[1] Discussed further in Question 2, p.18.

the Gulf War asking for our prayers, but rather carefully omitting to ask prayer for the people of Kuwait!) It is hard not to think that the debate would have been different and much more constructive. As we ask ourselves, What do we ask? we engage with situations. If we withhold the will from seeking to discern and ask the good, we withhold the surrender of our wills to the will of the Father. If our wills are not engaged in our prayers, our wills will never be corrected and taught.

And now imagine a whole series of occasional litanies, not only on national crises but also on other things that engage us as a society. Praying all round the abortion question might be a better thing to do than having a simple collect-length prayer such as Taylor suggested. What about a litany for the political future of Europe, and Britain's place in it?

6. LITURGY AND PENANCE

We have seen how liturgy may trace through the three steps of moral thought and help us in each of them. Let me say something in conclusion that takes us a little further. A work that liturgy can do, which is fundamental to any Christian exercise of moral thought or moral teaching, is pronouncing forgiveness.

It is the very heart of the gospel that we are free to act only as we are forgiven and accept forgiveness; and if the church intends to take seriously the ordering of its moral commitments in a world where all is moral confusion, it must surely do so by declaring and claiming God's forgiveness; Otherwise the church will either be a moralizing, Pelagian church, or else afraid ever to proclaim its moral commitments out of sheer fear of Pelagianism, in which case it will have only an inward, mystical gospel.

Ramsey again draws our attention to a liturgical example that he found helpful, and that was the Orthodox liturgy for the second marriage of the divorced. He found this an excellent model of how, by pronouncing forgiveness, the church could both illuminate and teach the moral structure that surrounded marriage. I would like to take this thought further, and repeat a suggestion that I made some years ago that we need a service of the public reconciliation of the penitent.[1]

This could be the key that opened the locked door of our difficulties with 'scandal' in the church: not only the place of divorced and remarried people in the church, but the place of homosexuals in the church, the place of capitalists in the church, the place of everything that gives scandal and affront. Private confession has achieved much, no doubt, over the centuries. It has not achieved this, which is to articulate the church's public moral commitment, and to make the church at ease with its own members, who are, all of them, sinners in one way or another and some of them notorious sinners.[2]

Public Reconciliation
Imagine something like this: by New Year's Day candidates will apply to the bishop requesting to be admitted to the annual service of reconciliation. They will make a private statement of what it is they have done of which they are ashamed. This will be accompanied by a letter from the parish priest or equivalent pastor, who will give details of the counselling and pastoral care that have been given, and will indicate his or her view of whether the candidate displays a well-judged self-understanding penitence. Perhaps also a letter from a close associate or friend who will vouch for the account given of the circumstances, so that nothing material or important is left out. Applications will then be screened to weed out the exhibitionists, habituees, and over-tender consciences, and perhaps in some cases to recommend the candidate to have a year's more counselling.

[1] *Principles in the Public Realm* (O.U.P. 1982).
[2] Discussed further in Question 4, p.18.

Then, at the beginning of Lent, permission is given to the successful candidates, who will be asked thereupon to abstain from communion for the season, and will be invited to attend a service in the cathedral on Holy Saturday. At the service the names of the candidates will be read out and there will be a brief statement, agreed by the candidate and the bishop, about what the repentance is for—enough to make the thing not an empty gesture, but not enough to excite prurient curiosity. For example:

Michael Jones acknowledges before the people of God that he has been unfaithful to his wife, and asks God's forgiveness and the prayers of the community, that he may be strengthened to serve God in holiness from this day forward.

Penny Smith acknowledges before the people of God that she has been dishonest in her business dealings, and unfeeling to those who have worked with her as employees. She asks for God's forgiveness and the prayers of the community . . . and so on.

Whereupon the bishop will invite the congregation to affirm their welcome to these penitents, and, the congregation having declared that it will, he will pronounce forgiveness and lay hands on each in prayer.

Scandal is a problem of the public earthly existence of the church, an earthly existence which fails to refer in that 'formed' way to the work of God and seems discordant with it. Scandal is the public dissonance of the church's common life with the the work and the grace of God, and it can only be dealt with by public acts. But the true public act of the church is an act of liturgy. We have our other public forms of the church: we have parliaments and we have councils, and they serve us well enough, but we do not see the *esse* of the church in them. We see the *esse* of the church in its liturgy, where, brought to unanimity of mind and clarity of purpose, the church makes its formed reference together to the work of God to which it responds. That is why theological moralists may sometimes dare to express themselves in liturgical forms, without, I hope, appearing too intrusive to those whose terrain it is, just as it has long been understood that dogmatic theologians may express themselves in liturgical forms too. We need a new Cranmer to do for the church's moral vision what Cranmer did long ago for its doctrine.

7. QUESTIONS AND COMMENTS

The lecture was followed by a short period of discussion. The questions are as they were put. The answers have been slightly edited.

1.
Q. *In your examples you have drawn attention to the verbal dimensions of liturgy—preaching and texts. Could you apply the same analysis to the non-verbal dimensions of the liturgy?*

O'D. Speech is the point at which the moralist and the liturgist meet. Therefore speech is the natural point at which to undertake tasks together. How those steps might be symbolically expressed in action I cannot imagine, but I would be receptive to proposals.

2.
Q. *You spoke about a prayer for use after abortion. Do you think there ought to be a Funeral service after an abortion?*

O'D. I would need to ponder some of the wider implications, but I can see how such a thing could be a useful witness in the case of an abortion undertaken in good conscience, and could help to free the parents from residual guilt.

3.
Q. *I agree with what you are saying about the bowdlerization of scripture—but it seems to me that there are certain problems which mean that is not quite as easy as that. If there is a progression in scripture, not only in revelation but in moral understanding in the life of the body of Christ, then certain of the ethical stances in the old testament are not such as we would as christians wholly endorse, though we would try to understand them. For instance you mention Psalm 137 saying that in fairness to the psalm it should be read as a whole. Would you be happy to encourage people to sing Psalm 137 the whole way through? I think this would be a little difficult to do, unless you are going to be able within the service to stop and elaborate why you are doing this, which you can't do in a liturgy without disrupting proceedings.*

O'D I can see how someone might think Psalm 137 too difficult to take on unless the second lesson came from Luke 23. Our Anglican tradition of reading the Old Testament and the NT alongside one another is important here. It builds in the wider hermeneutic context bthat you need. But taking the first three verses of Psalm 137 and saying, Isn't it beautiful? when that beauty was conjured up by the author to lull you, so that you would feel the blow on the nose when he gave it you, that is being dishonest with him.

4.
Q. *I found what you said at the end about the service of reconciliation for the penitent both very thought-provoking and very helpful. The passage that sprung to my mind from scripture was Matthew 18, which is about reconciliation presumably. I would have thought that only the*

final category, in the three categories that Jesus gives us there, would be suitable for use, and indeed essential for use. I would go a long way with you there, and we should produce something like this. Indeed, if my memory serves me right something not too dissimilar was present in the early church. But I would be reluctant to bring it in wholesale, before stages one and two (of Matthew 18) had been gone through.

O'D   I quite agree with that. One of the things that Matthew 18 is telling us is that the first stage is under the protection of privacy, and what you can do there, you should do there. If the reconciliation takes place at that stage you don't need to go any further. What I have in mind is a situation where someone, having left his wife and lived with mistresses and having driven his children through rebellion into atheism, is still a worshipper at church Sunday by Sunday. Nothing that person ever does privately will ever make other Christians entirely trust him. There has to be a moment when the church can say, 'Here we have him with us again! The prodigal son, has returned!'

5.

Q.   There is another subtle way in which the ASB lectionary sometimes edits scripture. It came to me on a Sunday when the theme was 'Those in Authority' where both year one and year two take the Romans 13 approach to church and state and there's no real engagement with a different biblical approach such as you might get in bits of Acts, and Revelation. Now, I'm quite happy to have Romans 13 as at least one biblical approach to that question, but it's not the only biblical approach, nor in some ways the most useful one in some situations. This raises the question of allowing the Bible to be itself and allowing it to speak without editing it in some way, while at the same time using the Bible in the classical sense in the lectionaries.

O'D.   I agree with that. It is up to the preacher to set the lectionary readings in context.

A RESPONSE
by
Michael Vasey
(Member of the Liturgical Commission)

This study appears not long after the announcement that Colin Buchanan has been awarded a Lambeth D.D. for his work as a liturgist and publisher. C. H. Roberts in a fascinating essay shows how the complex relationship of the early Christian communities to Jewish and Greek society was reflected in the characteristics of their first books. '[T]he earliest [Christian] manuscripts were the product not of the book trade but of communities whose members included businessment and minor officials well used to writing . . . On the rapid circulation of literature among the churches and on its regular and public reading much of the coherence of the early Church must have depended.'[1] Grove Books would have been at home in the early church as a recognized part of its pastoral strategy and theological life. St.John's Gospel would have fitted into the usual 24 pages with only minor cuts, although the house tradition of misprints might have led to new directions in Christian thought. Athanasius' classic work *On the Incarnation* would also have been quite at home although only as that rarity, a double issue.

The influence of Grove books and the widespread sense that such *samizdat* pamphlets are not quite serious raise questions about how and where the church thinks theology is done. Behind each series lies an author-group committed to thinking and communicating. The underlying model is a group of disciples together seeking to confess the faith in unfamiliar territory. As a theological activity the writing of a Grove book bears some resemblance to the corporate theological activity that gives rise to liturgical forms. It is a comparison to which we shall return.

Oliver O'Donovan was the first chairman of the Ethics group, for some three years from 1973; the second (for the following three years or so) was John Gladwin, subsequently Secretary of the General Synod's Board of Social Responsibility, and now Provost of Sheffield. Recently both of them have publicly directed their attention to the liturgy of the Church of England. John Gladwin, in a widely noted Synod speech,[2] pressed for more thought about what understanding of the church's relation to society underlies the liturgy. Since then he has been asked to expand his comments in a short essay for the forthcoming book by the Liturgical Commission.[3] Oliver O'Donovan's lecture raises the complementary question of the role of the liturgy in forming the moral sense of the people of God.

[1] 'Books in the Ancient World', in P. R. Ackroyd and C. F. Evans (ed.) *Cambridge History of the Bible* (1970), vol. 1, pp.63, 64.
[2] *Proceedings of Synod* November 1991, pp.927-8.
[3] Michael Perham ed. *The Renewal of Common Prayer* (SPCK and CHP, 1993)

ASB and beyond

Both interventions are timely. They recognize that liturgical revision is an incomplete task of great seriousness. In the debates that gave rise to the Alternative Service Book 1980 a number of attitudes can be found. Some saw liturgical revision as incipient apostasy. Some, possibly including the Archbishops of the day, saw it more as a piece of tedious modernization, replacing the family car with a model that was less finely made but more practical. Others resisted the production of a book at all as aiming for an outdated permanence in a rapidly changing culture. R. C. D. Jasper, Chairman of the Liturgical Commission during the revision, seems to have seen ASB 1980 as a necessary stage in which the church, whose liturgical instincts had atrophied recovered its ability to function as a liturgical body. In *The Development of the Anglican Liturgy 1662-1980* he quotes with apparent approval W. H. Frere's view that liturgical reform in England would require 'a long period of authorized experiment' before the church would be in a position to form 'instructed judgements.'[1]

The ASB 1980 achieved a great deal in creating an approach to parish worship that has appropriated some of the gains of the Oxford Movement and respects the human realities of a modern congregation. However its very success has revealed how much has still to be done if the liturgical forms of the Church of England are to be authentic 'articulated, colourful and contoured' vehicles for Christian faith today.

While Synod is preoccupied with other matters and many people imagine that liturgical renewal has been achieved, the ground is being prepared for a deepening of the Church's worshipping life. While the official time scale for replacing the ASB by the year 2000 seems optimistic, the process of fashioning and forming a deeper and authentic response 'to what God has done' is well under way. The dimensions raised by Oliver O'Donovan and John Gladwin need to be carefully attended to in this process.

It may be helpful to identify some of the places at which this refashioning of Church of England worship is occurring. A series of seasonal resource books[2] is enabling a corporate and dramatic appropriation of the potent moments of the Gospel story. *Patterns for Worship*[3] gives belated recognition to some of the growth points in Church of England liturgical life. Diocesan Liturgical Committees—and, at a national level, PRAXIS— are giving a new priority to pastoral education in liturgy. In its essays on *The Renewal of Common Prayer* the Liturgical Commission is trying to refocus nostalgia, individualism and confusion by identifying a strategy that recognizes the formative power of liturgy for both individuals and the church. A working group set up by the House of Bishops to explore patterns of nurture and the catechumenate will look at how new Christians are to be formed in the faith, reopening an issue that has not been officially

---

[1] pp.86-87.
[2] *Lent, Holy Week, Easter; The Promise of His Glory;* Michael Perham (ed.) *et al. Enriching the Christian Year*
[3] CHP 1989. cf. Trevor Lloyd, Jane Sinclair and Michael Vasey *Introducing Patterns for Worship.* The various parts of *Patterns for Worship* are being or have been revised by the Liturgical Commission for possible authorization or commendation.

reviewed since the Reformation.[1] In Synod gentle revision of the Canons dealing with liturgical matters is seeking to create a more pastoral and flexible approach to liturgical regulation.[2] Ahead lies the probable revision of the main authorized services of the Church.

In Response . . .

Against this background, I enjoyed and welcomed Oliver's lecture for many different reasons.

Firstly, there was the sheer pleasure of hearing a familiar and perceptive voice on liturgical matters. In small ways he has had an impact on recent liturgical reform. His trenchant comments on the proposed revision of the ICET *Te Deum* shaped the British response to the proposed ELLC text and may have improved it at various points.[3] A passing comment on the strengths of the Christological section of the Athanasian Creed led to the responsive text that is now before Synod in *Affirmations of Faith*.[4] His comment on the partial vision of Christian political responsibility in the American baptismal questions, and on the need for this to have a Christological basis, led to a rephrasing in our own use of this text.[5]

Secondly, there is excitement at hearing Christian ethics expounded as a living out of the work of God in Jesus Christ.[6] This, of course, has implications for the liturgical choice of ethical material and may even throw light on the modern decline in the use of the Ten Commandments. The Reformers' use of the Commandments hardly set them in a Christological framework. The fine attempt by the ASB to remedy this has often been disregarded as unwieldy. There is an argument for learning from the Orthodox in their liturgical use of the Beatitudes. More work certainly needs to be done.

Thirdly, there is substantial agreement with Oliver on many points, such as the quality of the Episcopal Church's liturgical work, the need to frame baptismal rites with more theological and moral alertness, and the ethical potential of the postcommunion section of the eucharist. His comments on preaching—illuminating in their own right—point to a need to recover an understanding of preaching that takes seriously its liturgical context.[7] Here the experience of the Black Pentecostal tradition also points beyond a purely didactic understanding of preaching.[8]

[1] For recognition that this is not simply about fitting new believers into a predetermined church shape, see Robert Brooks and Michael Vasey, 'What is the relationship between formation and inculturation?' in David R. Holeton (ed.) *Liturgical Inculturation in the Anglican Communion* (Alcuin/GROW 1990) pp.23-26.

[2] For an exploration of what a more radical departure from the traditional 'legal' style of Anglican regulation might look like see Anthony T. Lewis 'The Case for Constitutional Renewal in the Church in Wales' in Norman Doe (ed.) *Essays in Canon Law* (University of Wales Press 1992) pp 175-190, cf. also particularly chapters 6 and 7.

[3] cf. *Making Women Visible* (CHP 1988, 1989) p.66.

[4] *Affirmations of Faith* GS1038 p.6, cf. *Patterns for Worship* p.134.

[5] *Affirmations of Faith* GS1038 p.9, cf. *Patterns for Worship* p.135.

[6] See *Resurrection and Moral Order* (IVP, Leicester 1986). For a brief and accessible summary see R. T. France and A. E. McGrath (ed.) *Evangelical Anglicans* (SPCK, 1993) pp.96-107.

[7] Note in particular Ian Bunting's fine discussion in *Preaching at Communion* (Grove Worship Series 78), also Y. Brilioth *Landmarks in the History of Preaching* (SPCK 1950) for its recognition of the evangelical hero, Charles Simeon, as a significant embodiment of the patristic understanding of liturgical preaching.

[8] cf. ed. Joel Edwards *Let's Praise Him Again* (Kingsway 1992) ch.3.

The comments on Ethical Lections point up one of a range of issues in evaluating lectionaries. This summer on holiday I noticed that the Roman Catholic three-year lectionary deliberately omits the fact that Ebedmelech was a eunuch[1], another example of 'texts that present real difficulties . . . avoided for pastoral reasons.'[2] However, noting such protective omissions is but one small part in the important theological task of evaluating lectionaries. *The Revised Common Lectionary*[3], currently being considered by the churches, itself reflects a major unresolved dispute about how the Church is to hear the Old Testament.

Public Reconciliation

With mention of a restored rite of Public Reconciliation Oliver returns, as he notes, to a theme he has addressed before. His inaugural lecture mentioned as possible candidates 'indifferent parents who were learning to get along with their children' and 'theologians who had seen the error of romantic idealistic theology!' Such a rite would make visible the Church's commitment to both forgiveness and moral reality. It would also illuminate modern controversy about absolution. So-called 'sacramental confession' is a conflation of spiritual direction and ecclesiastical discipline. A public rite of reconciliation would help Anglicans to see the difference between official, charismatic (prophetic), and liturgical absolution.

His proposals for this rite have, of course, a very substantial history in the Church's tradition. They follow closely the practice set out so vividly in the *Didascalia.*[4] For a model liturgical text one might turn to the Early Roman rite which places near the start of the Maundy Thursday liturgy a finely crafted petition for acceptance by the Archdeacon ('Venerable Bishop, the moment of grace has come . . .') followed shortly after by the bishop leading the penitents in a sort of liturgical conger through the assembly while he sings of the joy of the angels over sinners who repent.

High Profile Liturgy

Fourthly, I was delighted by his recognition that the 'generating of liturgical forms' is one of the primary theological actions of the church. This contrasts sharply with the low profile that liturgy has in Western academic theology. Christian liturgy is forged in the fire of human encounter with God in the Christian assembly. It deserves more respect both as a source of Christian understanding and as an activity that requires attention and resourcing. The significance of liturgy as one of the primary theological acts of the church is nowhere asserted more robustly or explored more

[1] Jer. 38.7—Year C, 20th Sunday in Ordinary Time. The text does not occur at all in the Revised Common Lectionary.
[2] *Lectionary for Mass: Introduction* (United States Catholic Conference 1982) section 76, p.31. cf. Eileen Schuller 'Some Criteria of the Choice of Scripture Texts in the Roman Lectionary,' in P. C. Finn and J. M. Schellman (ed.) *Shaping English Liturgy* (Pastoral Press 1990) pp.385-404.
[3] Consultation on Common Texts (The Canterbury Press 1992).
[4] *Liturgical Portions of the Didascalia* Sebastian Brock and Michael Vasey (ed.) (Grove Books 1982). For a careful discussion of the practice there described, see Karl Rahner *Theological Investigations* vol XV (Crossroad, NY 1982) pp.225ff.

insightfully than in Aidan Kavanagh's *On Liturgical Theology*.[1] Many would warm to his warnings about a church that shirks the violence and discipline of this corporate encounter with God and is transmuted to 'a sort of religious boutique in the suburbs.' (p.43)

For all its formative power and theological significance the framing of liturgy requires a style of working that runs counter to the expansive individualism of much modern theology. In my experience working on the Liturgical Commission has close similarities to belonging to a Grove authorgroup. Different realities are brought together. Courtesy, integrity, passion and humour play an important part in a corporate search for authentic expression of Christian faith. Just as Grove has owed much to Colin Buchanan's style of chairmanship, so the Liturgical Commissions on which I have served are much indebted to the chairmanship of Colin James. Theological learning and a disciplined attention to carefully crafted expressions of faith from different traditions are held together with a deep engagement with many aspects of human reality as modern people experience it. Liturgists can be simultaneously caricatured as theologically ignorant, fashion-driven trendies, and as out-of-touch antiquarians. Although I am aware of many failures and inadequacies my own experience has been very different. Perhaps most moving has been the sense of shared artistic discipline in a corporate encounter with God. Liturgy and ethics share in the beauty that sometimes emerges as a gracious God reshapes broken humanity.

[1] Pueblo 1984.